GET INFORMED, STAY INFORMED

#METOO MOVEMENT

Heather C. Hudak

CRABTREE
PUBLISHING COMPANY
WWW.CRABTREEBOOKS.COM

Author: Heather C. Hudak
Series research and development:
Reagan Miller
Editor-in-chief: Lionel Bender
Editor: Ellen Rodger
Proofreaders: Laura Booth,
Wendy Scavuzzo
Project coordinator: Petrice Custance
Design and photo research:
Ben White
Production: Kim Richardson
Print coordinator: Katherine Berti
Consultant: Emily Drew,
The New York Public Library

Produced for Crabtree
Publishing Company by
Bender Richardson White

Photographs and reproductions:
Alamy: p. 34–35
Dino Fracchia: p. 14–15
Idealink Photography: p. 25
Marmaduke St. John: p. 40–41
Shawn Goldberg: p. 8–9
Getty Images: p. 32–33
Alex Wong: p. 30–31
Bloomberg: p. 31
Brendan Smialowski/AFP: p. 36–37
Chelsea Guglielmino: p. 4–5
David McNew: p. 26
Justin Sullivan: p. 24–25
Kyodo News: p. 18–19
Phil Walter: p. 32
Steven Ferdman: p. 6–7
Vyacheslav Prokofyev: p. 20–21
Shutterstock: box icons, cover, heading
band, p. 10, 12–13, 22–23
A_Lesik: p. 28–29
Denys Prykhodov: p. 12
Filip Jedraszak: p. 7
GagliardiImages: p. 16–17
Joshua Rainey Photography:
p. 39 (top)
Kathy Hutchins: p. 27

rawpixel.com: p. 42–43
Saikat Paul: p. 38
Shawn Goldberg: p. 1
unslutproject: p. 29 (Emily Lindin,
UnSlut: A Documentary Film/
The Matriarchy Media, LLC)
Wikimedia Commons
Gage Skidmore: p. 39 (bottom)
Diagrams: Stefan Chabluk, using
the following as sources of data:
p. 10 Reuters Institute Digital News
Report; p. 13 Daniel Brocklebank, www.
fantomdan.co.za; p. 17 Making Caring
Common, Harvard Graduate School
of Education; p. 18 (top) Twitter, The
Telegraph newspaper; p. 18 (bottom)
NPR/Robert Wood Johnson Foundation/
Harvard T.H. Chan School of Public
Health; p. 20 Daniel Brocklebank,
www.fantomdan.co.za; p. 21 NBC
News/Survey Monkey; p. 26 Daniel
Brocklebank, www.fantomdan.co.za;
p. 33 Vox/Morning Consult; p. 36
www.telegraph.co.uk/news/world/
metoo-shockwave, Crimson Hexagon,
Facebook, Instagram, Twitter

Library and Archives Canada Cataloguing in Publication

Hudak, Heather C., 1975-, author
#MeToo movement / Heather C. Hudak.

(Get informed--stay informed)
Includes bibliographical references and index.
Issued in print and electronic formats.
ISBN 978-0-7787-4960-8 (hardcover).--
ISBN 978-0-7787-4971-4 (softcover).--
ISBN 978-1-4271-2120-2 (HTML)

1. Sex crimes--Juvenile literature. 2. Sex crimes--Prevention--
Juvenile literature. 3. Sexual harassment--Juvenile literature. 4. Sexual
harassment of women--Juvenile literature. 5. Women--Crimes against-
-Juvenile literature. I. Title. II. Title: Hashtag me too movement.

HV6556.H83 2018   j364.15′3   C2018-903039-9
                                             C2018-903040-2

Library of Congress Cataloging-in-Publication Data

Names: Hudak, Heather C., 1975- author.
Title: #MeToo movement / Heather C. Hudak.
Description: New York : Crabtree Publishing Company, [2019] |
Series: Get informed--stay informed | Includes bibliographical
references and index.
Identifiers: LCCN 2018033711 (print) | LCCN 2018035958 (ebook) |
ISBN 9781427121202 (Electronic) |
ISBN 9780778749608 (hardcover) |
ISBN 9780778749714 (pbk.)
Subjects: LCSH: Sexual abuse victims--Juvenile literature. | Sex
crimes--Prevention--Juvenile literature. | Sexual harassment--
Prevention--Juvenile literature. | Social movements--Juvenile
literature.
Classification: LCC HV6625 (ebook) | LCC HV6625 .H83 2019
(print) | DDC 362.88--dc23
LC record available at https://lccn.loc.gov/2018033711

Crabtree Publishing Company
www.crabtreebooks.com   1-800-387-7650

Printed in the U.S.A./102018/CG20180810

Published in Canada
Crabtree Publishing
616 Welland Ave.
St. Catharines, ON
L2M 5V6

Published in the United States
Crabtree Publishing
PMB 59051
350 Fifth Avenue, 59th Floor
New York, NY 10118

Published in the United Kingdom
Crabtree Publishing
Maritime House
Basin Road North, Hove
BN41 1WR

Published in Australia
Crabtree Publishing
3 Charles Street
Coburg North
VIC, 3058

CONTENTS

In 2017, women around the world began making headlines for breaking the silence about their personal experiences with **sexual harassment** and **abuse**. They began using #MeToo Twitter messages to share their stories on **social media** platforms. Within the first two weeks of the campaign, Twitter reported more than 1.7 million uses of the **hashtag** in 85 countries.

Sexual harassment and abuse affect millions of people across the United States. In fact, every 98 seconds an American is sexually **assaulted**. The threat of unwanted sexual gestures and comments, and even assault and **rape**, are a reality for people in all parts of the world—especially women.

> *My work started in support of Black and brown girls in the community in Alabama. And it grew to be about supporting Black and brown women and girls across the country. And beyond that it grew to be about supporting marginalized people in marginalized communities.*

Tarana Burke explaining in an interview with *YES!* magazine why she originally started the Me Too movement.

▲ Me Too movement founder Tarana Burke spoke at the #MeToo Survivors March & Rally on November 12, 2017, in Hollywood, California, U.S.

THE MAKING OF A MOVEMENT

Stories and incidents forming the background to the #MeToo issue are not new. They have been around since the beginning of time. However, they are making headlines now more than ever. You have likely seen posts on Twitter or Facebook that include #MeToo. It represents the Me Too **movement**, a global **campaign** in support of survivors of sexual harassment, assault, and abuse.

Me Too was first used in 2006 by youth worker Tarana Burke as a way to speak to young women of color from low-income communities who had survived sexual abuse. She wanted to help them find a way to heal from their experiences. She used the concepts of **empowerment** and **empathy** to let these women know they were not alone.

AFFECTING EVERYONE

In 2017, the movement expanded after numerous women broke their silence about sexual abuse and harassment in the workplace. Over time, the movement has come to mean different things to different people. It has grown well beyond its original intent and has reached people all over the world, regardless of their **gender**, class, race, age, and religion.

You likely have a lot of questions about the Me Too movement. You may even have experienced sexual harassment or abuse yourself, or know someone who has. If you are wondering what you can do to help, you first need to learn the facts and understand the impact of the movement so you can become an informed citizen.

Knowledge is power. In order to make good decisions and have a meaningful impact on society, you need to be informed about **current affairs** and important issues such as the Me Too movement. Our world is constantly changing and evolving. As events unfold, new facts, theories, and opinions come to light. Staying informed about the latest details ensures you are never left believing false facts and rumors that have been spread over time.

You may think only adults need to watch the news and pay attention to current affairs. However, being informed is everyone's responsibility, regardless of age. It helps you understand the world around you and the impact global events have on your life. When it comes to the Me Too movement, being informed can help you stay safe from unwanted sexual acts or know how to react if you find yourself in an unsafe situation. It can empower you to share your story and fight for better rights. It can help you find empathy for others who have experienced sexual harassment or abuse and understand their **perspective**.

JUST THE FACTS

Learning about a new topic is a daunting task. There is a lot of information about the Me Too movement and more details **emerge** every day. Start by learning about the **context** of the movement. When and why did it begin? Who is involved and what is their perspective? Look for reliable, fact-based information. Read about different perspectives so you can see all sides of the issue. Having a well-balanced view can help you make informed decisions. It is all part of being a lifelong learner.

THE CENTRAL ISSUES

Sexual harassment and abuse happen all the time, yet they often go unspoken. Why is the Me Too movement so powerful? Why are people choosing to come forward and share their stories now? How might this have an impact on society and the solutions people put in place for dealing with the problem? How does staying informed help us be part of the solution?

> "If you've been sexually harassed or assaulted write 'me too' as a reply to this **tweet**."
>
> American actress Alyssa Milano in a tweet encouraging people to speak up about their experiences

▲ U.S. movie producer Harvey Weinstein was arrested and charged with rape in May 2018. More sexual assault charges were later added.

▶ People are taking part in demonstrations all over the world to show their support for the Me Too movement. Participants at an event in Malmo, Sweden, wore T-shirts saying #MeToo.

2 HOW TO GET INFORMED

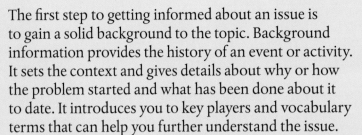

The first step to getting informed about an issue is to gain a solid background to the topic. Background information provides the history of an event or activity. It sets the context and gives details about why or how the problem started and what has been done about it to date. It introduces you to key players and vocabulary terms that can help you further understand the issue.

Once you have been exposed to a variety of sources, **interpretations,** and viewpoints, you can form more informed opinions about an issue. You can **engage** in conversations and debates, and take actions to improve your own life and the lives of others.

KEY INFORMATION

Gender equality happens when everyone, regardless of their sex, has the same rights, opportunities, and resources.

Misogyny is a hatred some men have toward women and girls, causing them to show prejudice against women and treat them in a way that is not fair or equal to how they treat men.

Sexual harassment happens when a person makes inappropriate comments and unwanted actions toward another person in a school, playground, workplace or professional setting, or even at home.

◄ In January 2018, protestors gathered at the city hall in Toronto, Canada, for the Women's March. It was part of a global event in support of women's rights.

GETTING STARTED

In today's world, there are four main types of information—written, visual, auditory (sound), and artifacts, or physical objects such as archaeological finds. There are also many different sources of information. Source materials include any documents, videos, paintings, photographs, Tweets, blogs, and interviews that help you learn about events in both the past and present.

CATEGORIES OF SOURCE MATERIALS

Primary sources are firsthand **evidence** of a topic—they were made by the people involved in or who witnessed the events. E-mails sent to a person that contain unwanted sexual comments are an example of a primary source. Diaries, photographs, audio recordings, tweets, and speeches are other examples.

Secondary sources are made by **analyzing**, interpreting, and **summarizing** primary source materials. A Hollywood movie based on personal stories and facts about the Me Too movement is an example of a secondary source. Biographies, newspaper and magazine articles written after an event takes place, and textbooks are other examples of secondary sources.

Tertiary sources are summaries of both primary and secondary sources. A Wikipedia article on Tarana Burke is an example of a tertiary source. Other examples include databases, **almanacs**, and encyclopedias.

Whenever you can, use primary sources. These are likely to be the most accurate and reliable.

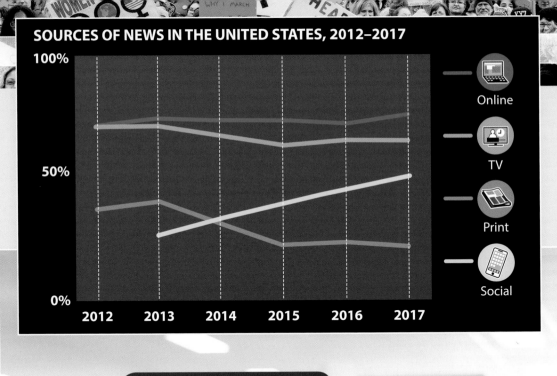

SOURCES OF NEWS IN THE UNITED STATES, 2012–2017

- Online
- TV
- Print
- Social

▼ When researching a topic, using print and digital material will give you a good range of views and perspectives.

INTERPRETING GRAPHICS

Graphics, or visuals, include charts, maps, and graphs—like the one shown opposite about shifts in sources of news. Graphics can help to make sense of complicated ideas. For example, there are many statistics about how often #MeToo is used on social media or which countries are using the hashtag. Putting the numbers on a map or in a bar graph can help provide perspective and show the magnitude of the issue. Refer to graphics to get informed.

> *I didn't tell anyone for, I think, seven years. I didn't know how to think about it. I didn't know how to accept it. I didn't know how not to blame myself, or think it was my fault. It was something that really changed my life. It changed who I was completely.*

American singer and songwriter Lady Gaga's 2015 interview with *Vanity Fair* magazine, in which she talks about being sexually assaulted at 19 years old by a man who was 20 years older than her.

The Internet and libraries are good places to look for high-quality sources of information. You may need to use key words and terms to find a broad base of information and ensure you get a global view of the issue. You can read blog posts, encyclopedias, and magazines, watch television news shows, listen to podcasts, and use research databases. Each of these source materials provides a unique mix of information and interpretations about a topic.

Some sources are based on fact, while others include personal opinions and summaries. Using the "Time and Place Rule" can help you judge the quality of source materials. According to this rule, sources created closer to the time of an event are more reliable and accurate. On this basis, a person who experiences an event firsthand is likely to be a far more reliable source of information than a person who reads about the event years later.

GETTING STARTED ON ME TOO

Good sources of information about the Me Too movement include:

- interviews by **credible** print, radio, and television reporters and journalists with people who have experienced sexual harassment
- evidence-based reports and **statistics** from governments about sexual harassment and abuse cases in countries around the world
- websites created by nonprofit groups dedicated to the Me Too movement and survivors of sexual harassment and abuse
- statements from politicians, survivors, and respected leaders on social media sites such as Twitter, Instagram, and Facebook.

Everyone has their own interpretation of a topic. Each person who analyzes a source comes at it with a different set of skills and experiences. These skills and experiences mold and shape their views and opinions. There is no one, right way to interpret a source. However, if you are not thorough in your research and analysis, you may interpret the information incorrectly.

ALLOWING FOR BIAS

Sometimes, the information people leave out of their story is just as important as the details they share. In other cases, people include bias in their source materials. Bias is when a person shows strong feelings in favor of or against something. In the case of the Me Too movement, many **emotions** are involved. It can be a challenge for people to keep their personal feelings out of their stories. How can you tell if a source is biased? Answers to these questions will help you determine any unwanted influences:

- Who created the source material? What was the person's age, race, religion, and job? Was the creator an expert on the topic? Was the whole story presented?
- When was the source created? How long after the event was it made? Is the source up to date, and, if not, what can it tell you about that time in history?

▶ Twitter is one of the most popular online news and social networking services. Users post and interact with messages known as tweets. From 2010 to 2017, more than 96 million tweets contained information related to the sexual harassment conversation. In October 2017, there was a sudden spike in Me Too messages.

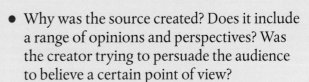

- Why was the source created? Does it include a range of opinions and perspectives? Was the creator trying to persuade the audience to believe a certain point of view?
- Who was the source created for? Who was the creator trying to reach with the message? Was it intended for a specific person or group of people?

Bias can be accidental or deliberate. When answering these questions, keep this in mind. Be sure to read a range of sources knowing that each may be trying influence your viewpoint or perspective.

◄ Always look at every source critically. Consider the point of view of the creator and check the facts and information presented against other sources of information to verify their credibility.

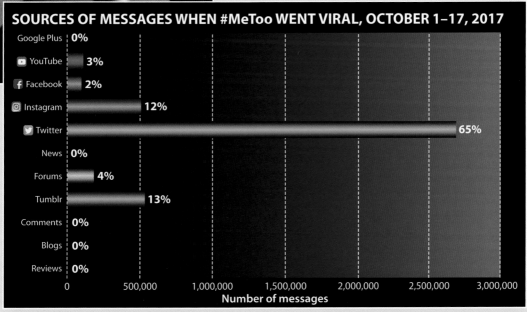

SOURCES OF MESSAGES WHEN #MeToo WENT VIRAL, OCTOBER 1–17, 2017

Source	Percentage
Google Plus	0%
YouTube	3%
Facebook	2%
Instagram	12%
Twitter	65%
News	0%
Forums	4%
Tumblr	13%
Comments	0%
Blogs	0%
Reviews	0%

Number of messages: 0 · 500,000 · 1,000,000 · 1,500,000 · 2,000,000 · 2,500,000 · 3,000,000

3 THE BIG PICTURE

Sexual harassment is any unwelcome sexual advances, requests for sexual favors, or any other verbal or physical acts of a sexual nature. It isn't a new thing and has been a pervasive, or widespread problem for a long time. Our interpretation of harassment has changed over time, as has society's acceptance of it. Recently, sexual harassment has been more widely recognized and condemned for what it is. While the Me Too movement started in the United States, the issues it presents are important to everyone—women, men, the **LGBTQ** community, and children.

ASK YOUR OWN QUESTIONS

Consider how an investigative journalist's five Ws and an H—who, what, where, when, why, and how—relate to the Me Too movement. Who is involved in the movement? What does it try to achieve? Where is it happening? When did it start and when might it end? Why does it matter? How might you find the answers to remaining questions?

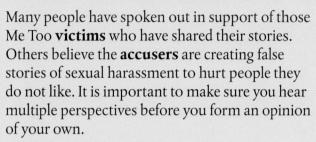

▼ Television networks play a key role is raising awareness of sexual harassment and the damage it does. For decades, many American television shows, such as *Mad Men, The Mary Tyler Moore Show,* and *The Office,* have used their popularity to highlight sexual harassment by portraying the issue on episodes of the shows.

Many people have spoken out in support of those Me Too **victims** who have shared their stories. Others believe the **accusers** are creating false stories of sexual harassment to hurt people they do not like. It is important to make sure you hear multiple perspectives before you form an opinion of your own.

IDENTIFYING THE ISSUE

In a class she was teaching in the mid-1970s, U.S. journalist and Cornell University professor Lin Farley asked female students about their personal experiences in the workplace. Farley found that every one of them had been forced to quit a job or had been fired for refusing to do sexual favors.

Farley looked to her work colleagues to put a name to her findings—to help make the stories real. They came up with the term "sexual harassment" and began fighting for social change. Soon, other women began to join the movement. They came forward with their own stories of sexual harassment in the workplace, which led to several high-profile court cases and new laws.

Over time, Farley's investigations and reports evolved into various initiatives that support victims of sexual harassment and abuse. Some, such as Silence is Violence and the Rape, Abuse, & Incest National Network (RAINN), provide **counseling** and other services to help victims deal with their experiences. The National Alliance to End Sexual Violence (NAESV) and others fight for changes to policies and laws on the issue.

While Tarana Burke was employed as a youth worker at a camp in the mid-1990s, a little girl opened up to her about how she had been sexually abused by her mother's boyfriend. Burke, who was raped for the first time at six years old, could not bear to listen to the girl's story. She stopped the girl from saying any more and sent her to speak with another counselor. As the girl walked away, two words repeated over and over in Burke's mind—"me too"—words Burke wishes she had told the girl instead of sending her away.

In 2006, Burke decided she could no longer allow another a girl of color, or any girl, to be silenced by her abuse. Burke started the nonprofit Just Be Inc. to help victims of sexual harassment and assault. She was looking for a motto that would help show empathy for women and girls who had survived sexual violence. The words "me too" came to mind. She decided they were the perfect words to connect with survivors and let them know they were not alone. She used after-school and youth-training programs to get the message out.

ME TOO GOES VIRAL

Burke was not looking for the words to become a banner, a campaign cry, or to "**go viral**" on social media. She was simply looking for a **catchphrase** survivors could use with one another to help them heal. However, that all changed in late 2017, when actress Alyssa Milano encouraged people everywhere to use #MeToo on social media. The hashtag soon exploded, gaining instant global attention.

WHAT'S AT STAKE?

Why are people so much more concerned about gender equality and sexual harassment today than ever before? What changed to make more people come forward and lend their voice to the movement? What other initiatives work for better rights with regard to sexual harassment and abuse?

> *First time I can remember being sexually assaulted I was nine years old. I told no one and lived with the shame and guilt thinking all along that I, a nine-year-old child, was somehow responsible for the actions of a grown man.*

American actress America Ferrera shared her own story of sexual assault on Instagram in 2017

SURVEY OF TEEN'S AND YOUNG ADULT'S SEXUAL EXPERIENCES

Touched without permission by a stranger	41%
Insulted with sexualized words by a woman	42%
Insulted with sexualized words by a man	47%
Having a stranger say something sexual to them	52%
Being catcalled	55%
Having a stranger tell them they are "hot"	61%

Based on survey of 3,000 college students in the U.S. in 2017

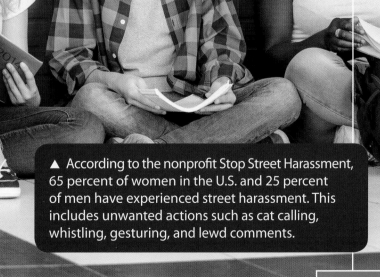

▲ According to the nonprofit Stop Street Harassment, 65 percent of women in the U.S. and 25 percent of men have experienced street harassment. This includes unwanted actions such as cat calling, whistling, gesturing, and lewd comments.

COUNTRIES WHERE THE #MeToo HASHTAG WAS MOST USED, OCTOBER 2017

United States	
United Kingdom	
Canada	
India	
Australia	
France	
Sweden	
Germany	
South Africa	
Colombia	

0% 10% 20% 30% 40% 50%

▼ #MeToo is used worldwide. In Japan, female opposition lawmakers used the hashtag while they protested the alleged sexual harassment of a female reporter by a top leader with the nation's finance ministry.

GENDER DISCRIMINATION: RESULT OF A SURVEY OF WOMEN IN THE U.S., 2017

37% Sexual harassment

29% Threats or non-sexual harassment

21% Violence

Percentage of 3,453 women who say they or a relative have experienced gender discrimination

> *...we need a shift in culture so that every single instance of sexual harassment is investigated and dealt with. That's just basic common sense.*
>
> Tarana Burke

In October 2017, numerous accusations of sexual harassment, violence, and gender inequality began to sweep through Hollywood. Several female celebrities, including American actresses Ashley Judd and Rose McGowan, and Italian actress Asia Argento, accused movie producer Harvey Weinstein of sexual harassment and abuse. Argento was later accused of sexual assault.

By spring 2018, more than 50 women had made claims against Weinstein. Television journalist Charlie Rose, Academy Award winning actor Kevin Spacey, American Idol host Ryan Seacrest, and actor James Franco were just a few of the other men in the entertainment industry accused of sexual harassment, assault, or abuse. The ripple effect extended beyond Hollywood to other high-profile leaders.

REINFORCING THE IDEA

On October 15, 2017, Alyssa Milano, one of McGowan's friends and former costars, took to Twitter in support. A friend suggested Milano encourage women to speak out by using #MeToo on social media. More than 645,000 replied to Milano's tweet. (See graphs on pages 13 and 20 showing the facts and figures.)

While Milano is often credited as the founder of the Me Too movement, she just helped make it popular. She had no knowledge of Burke's work when she used #MeToo on Twitter. Two days after sending out the now-famous tweet, Milano contacted Burke to see how they could work together to give power to the movement. Milano then went on the television show *Good Morning America* and explained how Burke's work puts the focus on survivors and gives them a voice rather than putting **perpetrators** in the spotlight.

To date, much of the Me Too movement has focused on Hollywood, since people in the entertainment industry tend to have a lot of power and many followers. But as the Me Too movement continues to grow in scope and size, so have the number of victims coming forward from all types of industries around the world. Politicians, Olympic athletes, chefs, businesspeople, hotel workers, and others have all started to share their stories, too.

REASSESSING THE SITUATION

Thanks in large part to the power of online platforms, the Me Too movement has increased awareness of sexual harassment and abuse. Recently, though, there has also been a growing backlash to, or reaction against, Me Too. Some people believe reports of gender inequality or sexual harassment are exaggerated or think the movement has gone too far.

KEY PLAYERS

Mónica Ramirez is the Board President of Alianza Nacional de Campesinas, the first female farmworkers' organization in the United States. She has spent more than 20 years promoting gender equality and finding ways to eliminate gender-based violence. In 2018, she was one of many activists invited to walk the red carpet at the Golden Globe Awards in support of political causes.

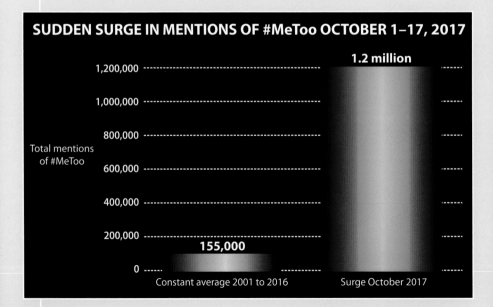

SUDDEN SURGE IN MENTIONS OF #MeToo OCTOBER 1–17, 2017

Total mentions of #MeToo

1,200,000 — **1.2 million**
1,000,000
800,000
600,000
400,000
200,000 — **155,000**
0

Constant average 2001 to 2016 — Surge October 2017

Others think individuals should have challenged their harassers at the time, or gone straight to their teachers, bosses, or the police after an incident. The issue is constantly changing.

The movement has sparked other campaigns, such as Time's Up, which seeks to end sexual harassment and abuse in the workplace. Sites such as *ihollaback.org* provide victims with a forum where they can share their stories without judgment and receive **validation** from others. Google's *Me Too Rising* shows how the Me Too movement is taking shape across the globe.

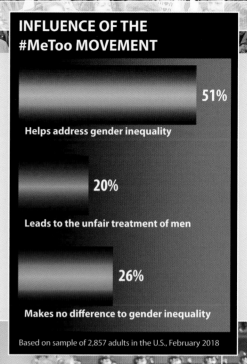

INFLUENCE OF THE #MeToo MOVEMENT

51%
Helps address gender inequality

20%
Leads to the unfair treatment of men

26%
Makes no difference to gender inequality

Based on sample of 2,857 adults in the U.S., February 2018

◀ In 2018, Israeli singer Netta Barzilai won the Eurovision Song Contest with a song inspired by the Me Too movement. The lyrics include *"I'm not your toy."*

4 FORMING AN OPINION

Information is all around us, but it is not always accurate or reliable. In many cases, information is unfiltered and unedited. Anyone can post articles online. It is important to make sure you thoroughly understand an issue before drawing conclusions about it. To do this, you need to develop information literacy skills. These skills help you know when you need more information on a topic, where to find it, how to **evaluate** and analyze it, and how to use it.

▶ Much of the information we come across is poor quality—it contains myths or outdated facts. It can lead you to draw incorrect conclusions, make poor decisions, and become **skeptical.**

> *If we can raise consciousness and really help create change, that's what's going to change this industry and change society. So I'm so sad that I have to talk about these issues, but it would be, I would be remiss not to.*

American actress Reese Witherspoon spoke about her first experience with sexual abuse at the age of 16 at *ELLE*'s Women in Hollywood event on October 17, 2017

WHAT'S AT STAKE?

Why is it important to develop information literacy skills? What can happen if people believe all the information they come across without evaluating it first?

QUALITY VERSUS QUANTITY

Information literacy skills are essential for navigating Internet sites, special interest group reports, magazine articles, and other sources to find valid, authentic information of good quality.

You might think having more information is better, but that is not necessarily the case. If you do not have quality information, the quantity does not matter. Information literacy is the basis of lifelong learning. By acquiring the tools you need to search for quality content, you can thoroughly **investigate** and understand an issue.

DEVELOPING YOUR SKILLS

Follow these information literacy guidelines for the Me Too movement to start developing your skills:

- Identify the type of information you need. Then, come up with questions that are clear, measurable, and concise such as, "How many people are sexually assaulted each year in the United States?"
- Locate sources of information that can help answer your questions such as government statistics and polls about sexual harassment and abuse. Be sure to use a wide range of sources from many varied perspectives.
- Evaluate each source critically to see if it is reliable and relevant. Consider who made it, when it was made, who it was made for, if it contains bias, or if any details were left out.
- Use the information in a meaningful way such as giving a presentation about how the Me Too movement started.

The Me Too movement draws attention to an issue that society has always had to face. It does this by making us look at how people treat each other, especially in relationships where one person has more power than the other. It also makes us question outdated and unfair ways of doing things. It is starting discussions about gender equality and rights and sparking changes in government and business policies, or rules. However, there are many different perspectives on the issue.

HOLLYWOOD PERSPECTIVE

At the start of the movement, actresses and musicians told how they had been groped or sexually assaulted by movie producers and actors. Others talked about how they had been promised movie roles in exchange for sexual favors. Some said they had been threatened—told they would have no career at all if they did not comply.

Together, the victims demanded justice. Entertainment studios responded by taking actions against the inappropriate—and illegal—behaviors of the accused. Many of the perpetrators have been removed from their jobs.

Gender equality and diversity are not new issues in the entertainment industry. For years, women and LGBTQ celebrities have shared their thoughts on these topics. They are underrepresented and underpaid across the industry. This is also true of politics, finance, and work in general around the world. Hollywood actresses are often asked to lose weight to portray perfection, or take off their clothes for roles. LGBTQ actors are often overlooked, stereotyped, or treated poorly. Most men in the movie industry do not always experience these issues.

KEY PLAYERS

In 2017, *Time* magazine honored Ashley Judd, Taylor Swift, and the hundreds of other women who came forward to share their stories of sexual harassment and violence. Collectively known as the Silence Breakers, they were named the "person of the year" for helping to spark a massive cultural transformation—the Me Too movement. Their bravery inspired other women who fight for rights and justice, such as Isabel Pascual, a strawberry picker; Susan Fowler, a political lobbyist; and Adama Iwu, a Silicon Valley engineer, to lend their voices to the cause.

▶ At the 2018 Professional Business Women of California (PBWC) event, actress Ashley Judd (second from right), and We Said Enough cofounder Adama Iwu (far right) held a panel discussion about Me Too.

#MeToo #TimesUp:
A Defining Moment
in History for Women

▲ At the 2018 Cannes Film Festival in France, Australian actress Cate Blanchett, Burundian singer Khadja Nin, and 82 women working in the movie industry gathered on the red carpet . They protested the lack of female filmmakers honored throughout the history of the festival.

WHO SENT #MeToo SOCIAL MEDIA MESSAGES OCTOBER 1–17, 2017

Women 71%

Men 29%

▼ Often, men are not sure how to respond to the Me Too movement. In October 2017, they accounted for only 29 percent of the key #MeToo conversation.

#TRUST
#RESPECT
#MYMOM
#MYWIFE
#MYDAUGHTERS
#MYSISTERS

#MeToo

THE CENTRAL ISSUES

Many men express concerns about how to approach women. They are unsure of how to handle a conversation or give a compliment. Some men feel they need to avoid women to prevent any potential issues. How can men and women work together in such cases? How is this a setback for women in the workplace? Sexual violence has an impact on men as well as women. In fact, 1 in 10 rape victims is male.

▼ Crews has said he empathizes deeply with the women and members of the LGBTQ community who choose not to break their silence. He hopes by telling his story he can help harassers think twice about their actions and how they make people feel afraid.

Many men want to help the movement but worry how their efforts will be received. They wonder what they may have said or done to **offend** someone that could be seen as harassment and how they should behave in the future. Some fear being falsely accused.

Many celebrities have spoken in support of their peers. Actors Bryan Cranston and Jeff Goldblum are just a few who have said they are **reflecting** on their own past behaviors and making sure all of their relationships are respectful. Actor Sean Penn and life coach Tony Robbins have suggested women want to destroy men's careers by saying they were harassed. Robbins later apologized, saying he agreed with the movement's goals. *Scream* actor David Arquette and *Friends* star David Schwimmer have urged men to help prevent sexual harassment and abuse from happening in the first place.

MEN RESPOND

Though cases of sexual harassment and abuse against men are less common, it does not mean they do not occur. Many men choose not to come forward. They are **embarrassed** and think others will look down on them or make fun of them. But more men are choosing to speak out, thanks to the Me Too movement. Actor and former National Football League star Terry Crews is one of those.

Inspired by the Me Too movement, Crews decided to tell his story in a series of tweets on October 10, 2017. At an event in 2016, he was assaulted by a high-level Hollywood executive. The man later called to apologize, and Crews accepted out of fear. He was worried people would punish him or that he would end up in jail.

Sexual harassment and violence can take place anywhere—in the workplace, at home, on a bus, in a movie theater, at school, or any other setting. It happens more often than anyone knows. Often women do not tell their stories. They feel they may lose their jobs and their credibility. Some worry they will not be believed. As more and more women share their stories, there is strength in numbers. By speaking out, women can help produce change and work toward fair and just workplaces and societies where everyone is a valued member.

Women around the world can relate to and identify with the experiences brought into focus by the Hollywood actresses who have used their power and **prestige** to gain international attention. They have been inspired to share their own stories, take action, and demand changes.

THE CENTRAL ISSUES

#MeToo has been very popular and many people have used it around the world. What happens when the media moves on to a new stories? Will people keep using the hashtag to tell their story? Why is it important to do more than just talk about the issue? What can you do to help keep the movement going?

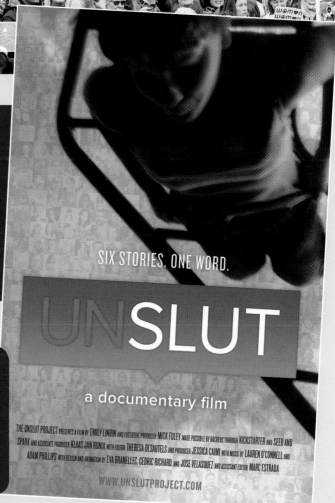

SIX STORIES. ONE WORD.

UNSLUT

a documentary film

THE UNSLUT PROJECT PRESENTS A FILM BY EMILY LINDIN AND EXECUTIVE PRODUCER MICK FOLEY MADE POSSIBLE BY BACKERS THROUGH KICKSTARTER AND SEED AND SPARK AND ASSOCIATE PRODUCER KLAAS JAN RUNIA WITH EDITOR THERESA DESAUTELS AND PRODUCER JESSICA CAIMI WITH MUSIC BY LAUREN O'CONNELL AND ADAM PHILLIPS WITH DESIGN AND ANIMATION BY EVA BRANELLEC, CEDRIC RICHARD, AND JOSE VELASQUEZ AND ASSISTANT EDITOR MARC ESTRADA

WWW.UNSLUTPROJECT.COM

▶ The UnSlut Project was started by Emily Linden who, at age 11, was branded a slut and bullied as a result. Using her diaries from the time as evidence, she produced a book and documentary to help victims of sexual harassment deal with abuse.

▼ Professional cheerleaders often experience sexual harassment as part of their job. It is not uncommon for people to make sexual comments to cheerleaders or even grope them.

NEXT STEPS

Tarana Burke did not think there would be a time when sexual violence would be a nationwide conversation. Now that it is, she believes the time to talk is over. Burke wants to shift the movement from talking about the issue to **strategizing** about the changes that need to be made. She wants to focus less on negativity and getting out the names of perpetrators and instead start making progress on creating new policies and providing resources to survivors.

Burke is worried about what will happen as the movement fades from the **media** and popularity dies down. She wants to keep the conversation alive by putting the voices of women who have experienced harassment and assault in the news. She is thankful for the publicity and the funds Me Too has raised, but now she wants to take the movement to a new level.

A survey by the Canadian government showed 40 percent of office workers who had made sexual harassment claims said their employer did nothing to resolve the issue. Thanks to the Me Too movement, many businesses are starting to think about their responsibility to prevent and protect employees from sexual harassment. Some have clear rules that say these attitudes and behaviors will not be tolerated. But they rely on people coming forward.

Some businesses think that because people have not come forward it means they do not need to take action. Others are taking a more **proactive** approach—just because no one has made a claim to date does not mean sexual harassment is not happening. To protect their employees from unwanted sexual acts, many businesses are establishing what is—and what is not—acceptable behavior in the workplace.

MAKING CHANGES

Businesses are developing new policies or updating existing policies to ensure they align with sexual harassment laws. They are clearly outlining appropriate actions and steps to take in the event of a claim. They are also providing employees with training so they have a solid understanding of what is expected of them. The goal is to prevent incidents from occurring, as well as prevent potential lawsuits and negative press geared toward their companies.

In general, businesses are becoming more aware of the issue and are taking action more quickly. All companies, big or small, are held to the same legal standards when it comes to sexual harassment—and must investigate a claim and take the appropriate corrective actions.

LOW RISK   HIGH RISK

WHAT'S AT STAKE?

How has reading about different people's and support groups' perspectives influenced or changed your understanding of the issue? What evidence for sexual harassment do you think is the strongest? Why do you think this?

◀ According to a survey in Canada, 94 percent of adult workers asked believed sexual harassment was not a problem in their workplace. However, it seems 80 percent of harassment cases go unreported.

▼ Modern factories with large numbers of workers, such as this smartphone manufacturer in Texas, have guidelines and rules that are supposed to stop sexual harassment

Around the world, the Me Too movement is sparking a political revolution. Women make up 90 percent of sexual assault survivors. Still, there are too few women in positions of political power to bring about change in government policies and **legislation** on the issue.

The concept of a democracy suggests all people should have an equal voice and fair representation in the government. As a result, more women are starting to run for political offices in the hope of disrupting the **status quo**.

Canadian Prime Minister Justin Trudeau has said stronger legislation is needed in government workplaces, but that it will take time to **implement**. In the meantime, organizations such as the Young Women's Leadership Network have developed on online tools to help. These tools were made to prevent the sexual harassment and abuse of volunteers helping with campaigns. The hope is that women will remain involved in politics rather than leaving if an uncomfortable or dangerous situation occurs.

▲ Jacinda Ardern, the prime minister of New Zealand, is a strong supporter of equal rights for women and the LGBTQ community. She made headlines in 2018 for having a baby while leader of a country—the first leader to do so since Pakistan's Benazir Bhutto in 1990.

DEMOCRATS V. REPUBLICANS

In the United States, the Democratic and the Republican perspective on sexual harassment vary widely. In 2018, Pew Research Center polled the opinions of 6,251 people about workplace sexual harassment. The results show 62 percent of Democrats see men getting away with sexual harassment as a major problem. By contrast, only one in three Republicans feel the same way. Earlier, Pew asked people if they thought the country had done enough to support equal rights for women. While 69 percent of Democrats said they thought the country could do more, only 26 percent of Republicans agreed.

ASK YOUR OWN QUESTIONS

Do you think the U.S. government could do more to stop sexual harassment and abuse? What changes can the government make to help give women a stronger voice?

▲ U.S. president Barack Obama addressed Canada's House of Commons on Parliament Hill during the North American Leaders' Summit on June 29, 2016. Women make up only 26 percent of Canada's federal government.

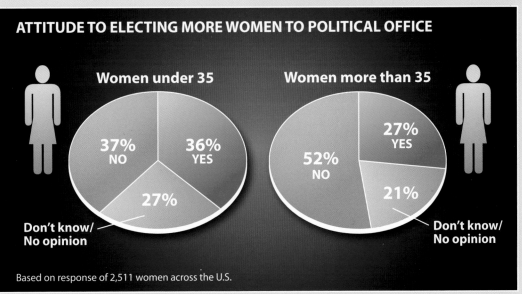

ATTITUDE TO ELECTING MORE WOMEN TO POLITICAL OFFICE

Women under 35

37% NO

36% YES

27%

Don't know/ No opinion

Women more than 35

27% YES

52% NO

21%

Don't know/ No opinion

Based on response of 2,511 women across the U.S.

5 STAYING INFORMED

Facts, information, and opinions about the Me Too movement change often. As more people express their views and new evidence is introduced, perspectives shift. People who have spoken out against Me Too or supported it in the past may not feel the same way in the future as they learn new information.

New source materials also include misinformation and bias. False details and personal opinions spread easily across the Internet. People are often quick to share stories and express their personal points of view on social media without becoming thoroughly informed about the issue. Reading widely and keeping up to date ensures you have a balanced view.

ASK YOUR OWN QUESTIONS

Why would a person tell lies or create myths about the Me Too movement? Do they always do it on purpose? Who benefits from sharing false information? How can you help prevent the spreading of inaccurate posts?

◀ A 2014 survey of 1,400 middle school kids done by the University of Illinois at Urbana–Champaign showed that at least one in four students have experienced sexual harassment or abuse on school grounds.

SPECIFIC ME TOO SOURCES

If you think a source seems unreal or includes errors, check its information against other sources to make sure they agree and are consistent. Find out if the content creator is an expert on the issue or if facts have been used to support any ideas and opinions being shared.

Some good specific source materials for sexual harassment and the Me Too movement will be found at:

- government and international policy and awareness websites such as the Government of Canada: Is it Harassment? page, UN Women, and the U.S. Equal Employment Opportunity Commission
- nonprofit groups such as RAINN, Me Too, Time's Up, and Stop Street Harassment
- documentaries and truth-based movies about real-life stories of sexual abuse such as *Out in the Night, Don't Tell Anyone,* and *Hooligan Sparrow*
- look for podcasts and blog sites created by sexual harassment experts and organizations, victims of sexual harassment and abuse, and people who do not share your own point of view on the topic
- read biographies, such as *I am Malala: The Girl Who Stood Up for Education and Was Shot by the Taliban* by Christina Lamb and Malala Yousafzai, *Speak: The Graphic Novel* by Laurie Halse Anderson, and *The Confidence Code for Girls: Taking Risks, Messing Up, and Becoming Your Amazingly Imperfect, Totally Powerful Self* by Claire Katty Kay and Claire Shipman.

#MeToo SOCIAL MEDIA ACTIVITY OCTOBER–NOVEMBER 2017

Circle size represents total social media messages, October 14 to November 6

KEY INFORMATION

• Half of all working women have been sexually harassed at work.

• About 50 percent of men think women are well represented in the workplace in companies where only 10 percent of the leaders are women.

• More than 30 percent of countries around the world do not have laws protecting women against sexual harassment.

• About 25 percent of American women will be sexually assaulted at some point in their lives.

> *From Latin America to Europe to Asia, on social media, on film sets, on the factory floor and in the streets, women are calling for lasting change and zero tolerance for sexual assault, harassment and discrimination of all kinds.*
>
> From United Nations (UN) Secretary-General António Guterres's speech on International Women's Day in 2018

◄ The organization Peace Over Violence hosts Denim Day in April each year as a way to honor Sexual Violence Awareness Month. In 2018, rapper Maya Jupiter performed at the event in support of the cause.

At first, the Me Too movement was about creating a community of people who have survived sexual violence and letting them know they are not alone. It grew out of a need for resources for survivors, particularly young women of color in **underprivileged** communities. Over time, it has expanded to a global conversation about sexual violence and the needs of survivors from all backgrounds and cultures, regardless of race, gender identity, status, religion, or skin color.

Soon after the Me Too movement began, 300 women in the film, television, and theater industries created the Time's Up campaign to take action against sexual harassment in the workplace. In just 60 days, Time's Up raised more than $21 million. The money is being used to help women pay for legal support in sexual harassment cases. More than 1,700 women from all types of jobs and backgrounds have asked Time's Up for help.

SPEAKING OUT

As more people come forward to share their personal stories of sexual harassment and abuse, it is having a huge impact on society. Until now, many people have felt they could not speak out. They thought they would be punished in some way or that no one would believe them. Now, more than ever, people are starting to feel that their stories are being heard and believed.

To date, women in 85 countries have tweeted their support for the Me Too movement. Outside of North America, many nations have come up with their own local translation for the hashtag, such as #YoTambien in Spain, #BalanceTonPorc in France, and #QuellaVoltaChe in Italy.

Today, the Me Too movement is about creating cultural change. It looks to survivors to speak out and to find ways to end sexual violence in their own communities and workplaces. The ultimate goal is to disrupt, or alter the systems in society such as education, government, law, and religion that allow sexual harassment and violence to happen. Another aim is to hold harassers **accountable** for their actions and end sexual violence.

STAY ALERT

It is important to realize that sexual harassment and abuse can happen to anyone, any place, at any time. Many young people experience sexual harassment or trauma at school or at home. In fact, statistics show that 1 in 4 girls and 1 in 6 boys experience sexual abuse by the age of 18. The abusers may be their parents, guardians, teachers, relatives, or friends. What starts off as inappropriate comments and jibes can develop into physical and mental abuse.

WHAT YOU CAN DO

Many celebrities have used their fame to draw attention to the Me Too movement. But there are things you can do to help support such a cause or stand up against it, too. You can write to politicians demanding changes to legislation. You can host an event that draws awareness to sexual harassment and abuse. You can volunteer for an organization that supports survivors. You can even ask your school to include teaching about respectful behavior as part of its lesson plans.

Writing a blog, recording a podcast, and sharing fact-based information on social media are other ways you can help. But be sure to consider all points of view.

WHAT'S AT STAKE?

What would you do if a friend at school was being sexually harassed? Who would you turn to, and what would you say? Find out if your school has a policy and procedure in place to deal with the issue.

▲ Women all over the world have protested sexual harassment in the streets of their cities and in front of their governments.

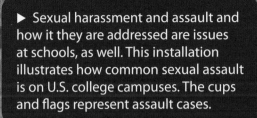

▶ Sexual harassment and assault and how it they are addressed are issues at schools, as well. This installation illustrates how common sexual assault is on U.S. college campuses. The cups and flags represent assault cases.

3,250 students

On a campus our size, according to national statistics, 3,250 students experience sexual assault during their time in college. That's 1 in 5 women and 1 in 16 men.

(National Sexual Violence Resource Center, 2015)

KEY PLAYERS

Anita Hill is a U.S. attorney and law professor. In 1991, she was called to testify against her former employer, Clarence Thomas, in a sexual harassment case. Thomas had been nominated for a position as a Supreme Court judge. Hill hoped her testimony would prevent him from being appointed to the position, but it did not. However, following her testimony, anti-sexual harassment legislation was passed, more women than ever before ran for office, and thousands of sexual harassment claims were filed. Today, Hill is seen as a national symbol for the Me Too movement.

6 PLAN OF ACTION

Getting informed involves building a solid understanding of a subject. Staying informed requires constantly monitoring the news and being alert for new developments. The Internet provides a constant flow of new information from across the globe. However, many websites include outdated, biased, or false information that can have a negative impact. Always consider bias, context, and different perspectives.

SEARCH TIPS

When looking at websites, address extensions can help pinpoint what sort of information you may be getting.

.gov (government)—restricted to use by government entities.

.org (organization)—anyone can register for this, although it is often used for nonprofit organizations and charities.

.com (commercial)—originally for businesses, it is the most widely used extension.

Country extensions:
.ca Canada
.au Australia
.uk United Kingdom
.ru Russia
.de Germany

▼ Millions of #MeToo supporters took part in protests across the globe on January 20, 2018, as part of the Women's March.

YOUR NEWS DIET

Make sure to look beyond your social media newsfeed or your favorite blog site to find out what others are saying about issues. Having a well-balanced **news diet** can help you better understand the impact issues such as the Me Too movement have on you and on people living in other parts of the world. Follow the work of nonprofit organizations, look for recent statistics and survey results, and listen to the stories of survivors to stay informed about Me Too.

Use these sources and guidelines:

- Read major newspapers and magazines, such as *Time, The New York Times, The Wall Street Journal,* and *USA Today.* Check out critical publications for young people, such as girlslife.com
- Talk with friends, family, and teachers about current affairs. Be open to new and different perspectives.
- Set up a Google alert for news stories about the Me Too movement, so you always have the latest information.
- Watch TV documentaries about the topic.
- Listen to radio interviews, panels, and discussions with workers, employers, business leaders, and politicians about Me Too issues.
- Read brochures containing facts and information about sexual harassment and abuse that you may find at your doctor's office, at a drugstore, or in the office of your school guidance counselor.
- Stream fact-based news media on the Internet such as the Cable News Network (CNN) and National Public Radio (NPR).

Be sure to fact check any information you find about the Me Too movement, especially if you are using the Internet as your main source. Watch for typos, **clickbait**, and a large number of ads on the sites you visit. Any of these clues may indicate the information on the site is not reliable or well researched. Use sites such as Snopes and WhoWhatWhen to determine if the information you are reading is fact or fiction. Performing a Google search can also help you weed out fake news. Search for a topic then search again using different keywords or phrases to see what Google suggests.

IF YOU NEED HELP

The time to act is now. No other time in history has been more focused on breaking the silence about sexual harassment and abuse. For change to happen, people everywhere need to keep the conversation going.

The Me Too movement is still going strong, but there is some fallout surrounding it. Not everyone is sympathetic to the issue and people have criticized the campaign. Think about what you can do to help draw more attention to the issue. What changes can you make in your own life? How can you help survivors of sexual harassment and abuse?

One of the most important things you can do is ask for help if you need it. You can reach out to share your story in many places that provide a safe, judgment-free environment, such as the National Sexual Assault Hotline or the National Child Abuse Hotline. School counselors and family doctors are other people you can talk to about your situation. You will find more sources of help on page 47.

▶ If a friend tells you they are being sexually harassed or abused, it is important to take action to make sure they are safe and get them out of the situation. Share the information with an adult you trust such as a parent or a teacher.

SEARCH TIPS

In search windows on the Internet:

• Use quotation marks around a phrase to search for that exact combination of words (for example, "street harassment")

• Use the word Define and a colon to search for word definitions (for example, Define: gender equality)

• Use a colon and an extension to search a specific site (for example, Workplace sexual harassment:.gov for all government websites that mention sexual harassment in the workplace)

> *And when that new day finally dawns, it will be because of a lot of magnificent women, many of whom are right here in this room tonight, and some pretty phenomenal men, fighting hard to make sure that they become the leaders who take us to the time when nobody ever has to say, 'me too' again.*

Oprah Winfrey, *Golden Globe* Award speech 2018

GLOSSARY

abuse Actions meant to harm or injure someone

accountable Taking responsibility for one's own actions

accusers People who claim another person has done something wrong

almanacs Annual publications with information about specific dates, events, or general topics

analyzing Studying or examining something carefully

assaulted Physically attacked

campaign A plan with a goal

catchphrase A word or phrase that is easy to remember and draws attention to something

clickbait Content that entices a person to click on a certain website or link

context Circumstances, background, or setting for an event, idea, or activity

counseling Advice or guidance provided by a professional

credible Able to be trusted or believed

current affairs Happening now

embarrassed Made to feel foolish

emerge Become known or apparent

emotions Feelings

empathy Being able to understand and share the feelings of others

empowerment Becoming more confident and stronger

engage Take part or get involved

evaluate Judge or determine the value of something

evidence Facts or information that prove if something is true or real

gender Having male or female characteristics based on cultural differences

go viral To spread quickly to many people on social media

hashtag A word or phrase with the # sign in front of it that is used to draw attention to a social media post

implement Put into effect

interpretations Explaining the meanings of something

investigate Carry out research to discover new information

legislation Laws made by a government

LGBTQ An acronym for lesbian, gay, bisexual, transgender, and queer, or questioning

media Methods of mass communication such as TV and radio

movement The act of people working together in support of advancing a cause

news diet The sources you use to get your news

offend To cause a person to feel hurt, annoyed, angry, or upset

perpetrators People who commit illegal or harmful acts

perspective Viewpoint

policies Ideas, plans, and procedures used to guide decision making

prestige To have a great deal of respect due to one's success or achievements

proactive Taking actions to control a situation and make changes before it happens

rape The illegal act of forcing a person to take part in a sexual act against his or her will

reflecting Thinking carefully and deeply about something

sexual harassment Unwanted sexual advances, requests for sexual favors, or other unwelcome sexual acts

skeptical Having doubts or not easily convinced

social media Websites and computer software that lets people communicate and share information

statistics A type of math that deals with the collection, analysis, and presentation of numerical data

status quo The way things currently are

strategizing Coming up with a plan for reaching a goal

summarizing Stating the main points briefly

tweet A post of information on Twitter

underprivileged Having fewer privileges or rights than many members of society

validation Recognition that a person's feelings are valid

victims People who have been harmed, attacked, or injured by someone else

SOURCE NOTES

QUOTATIONS

p. 5 www.cnn.com/2017/10/30/health/metoo-legacy/index.html

p. 7 https://twitter.com/alyssa_milano/status/919659438700670976?lang=en

p. 11 www.vanityfair.com/hollywood/2015/12/lady-gaga-shares-how-she-survived-her-sexual-assault

p. 16 www.latimes.com/entertainment/la-et-entertainment-news-updates-america-ferrera-me-too-sexual-assault-1508262986-htmlstory.html

p. 19 www.theguardian.com/world/2018/jan/15/me-too-founder-tarana-burke-women-sexual-assault

p. 23 www.thecut.com/2017/10/quotes-from-25-famous-women-on-sexual-harassment-and-assault.html

p. 36 www.un.org/press/en/2018/sgsm18921.doc.htm

p. 42 https://blog.simonsays.ai/oprah-winfreys-powerful-metoo-speech-as-she-receives-the-cecil-b-cc911977dffa

REFERENCES USED FOR THIS BOOK

Chapter 1: International Issue, pp. 4–7

www.cnn.com/2017/10/30/health/metoo-legacy/index.html

www.rainn.org/statistics/victims-sexual-violence

https://metoomvmt.org

www.bbc.com/news/entertainment-arts-41594672

www.quora.com/Why-is-it-important-to-read-listen-watch-the-news-and-stay-informed

http://archive.star.txstate.edu/node/743.html

Chapter 2: How to Get Informed, pp. 8–13

www.crk.umn.edu/library/primary-secondary-and-tertiary-sources

https://research.lib.buffalo.edu/research-tips/findingbackgroundinformation

http://ergo.slv.vic.gov.au/learn-skills/research-skills/select-resources/identify-bias

https://westernreservepublicmedia.org/history/analyze.htm

Chapter 3: The Big Picture, pp 14–21

www.huffingtonpost.ca

http://msmagazine.com/blog/2014/06/19/street-harassment-usa

http://fantomdan.co.za/metoo-stats-highlight-the-prevalence-of-sexual-assault-today

www.nytimes.com/2017/10/20/us/me-too-movement-tarana-burke.html

www.timesupnow.com

www.worldwithoutexploitation.org/co-chairs/monica-ramirez

www.alianzanacionaldecampesinas.org

Chapter 4: Forming an Opinion, pp. 22–33

www.mindtools.com/pages/article/newTED_00.htm

www.stevepavlina.com/blog/2010/06/suspending-judgment

www.cct.umb.edu/susjudgement.html

www.pennlive.com/news/2018/04/country_deeply_divided_on_impa.html

www.readingrockets.org/article/teaching-information-literacy-skills

www.nbcnews.com/politics/politics-news

www.hollywoodreporter.com/news

www.nytimes.com

www.independent.co.uk

www.bbc.com/news/business-43866590

https://metoomvmt.org

www.ggenyc.org/about

Chapter 5: Staying Informed, pp. 34–39

www.usnews.com/news

www.newsweek.com

www.timesupnow.com

http://time.com/5173213/jodi-kantor-metoo-weinstein-watermark-sexual-harassment-workplace

Chapter 6: Plan of Action, pp. 40–43

https://variety.com/2017/biz/news/anita-hill-uta-sexual-harassment-1202634689

www.factcheck.org/scicheck

www.wikihow.com/Find-if-a-Website-Is-Legitimate

www.themuse.com/advice/staying-current-get-global-news-the-right-way

www.makeuseof.com/tag/true-5-factchecking-websites

FIND OUT MORE

Finding good source material on the Internet can sometimes be a challenge. When analyzing how reliable the information is, consider these points:

- Who is the author of the page? Is it an expert in the field or a person who experienced the event?

- Is the site well known and up to date? A page that has not been updated for several years probably has out-of-date information.

- Can you verify the facts with another site? Always double-check information.

- Have you checked all possible sites? Don't just look on the first page a search engine provides.

- Remember to try government sites and research papers.

- Have you recorded website addresses and names? Keep this data for a later time so you can backtrack and verify the information you want to use.

WEBSITES

Get information, support, and advice about sexual harassment and abuse.
www.rainn.org

Find out more about the Time's Up movement.
www.timesupnow.com

Learn who the Silence Breakers are and read about their stories.
http://time.com/time-person-of-the-year-2017-silence-breakers

Find out how the Me Too movement is helping survivors and working to make changes.
http://metoo.org

BOOKS

La Bella, Laura. *Confronting Sexism*. Rosen Publishing Group, 2018.

Lindin, Emily. *UnSlut: A Diary and a Memoir*. Zest Books, 2015.

Patel, Sonia. *Rani Patel in Full Effect*. Cinco Puntos Press, 2016.

Schatz, Kate and Stahl, Miriam Klein. *Rad Women Worldwide*. Ten Speed Press, 2016.

Stone, Tanya Lee. *Almost Astronauts: 13 Women Who Dared to Dream*. Candlewick Press, 2009.

ABOUT THE AUTHOR

Heather C. Hudak has written hundreds of books for children. When she's not writing, Heather loves traveling and has been to more than 50 countries.

INDEX